Start with Art

Painting

Isabel Thomas

Heinemann Library
Chicago, Illinois

www.heinemannraintree.com
Visit our website to find out more information about Heinemann-Raintree books.

To order:
☎ Phone 888-454-2279
💻 Visit www.heinemannraintree.com to browse our catalog and order online.

Edited by Dan Nunn, Rebecca Rissman, and Catherine Veitch
Designed by Richard Parker
Picture research by Mica Brancic and Hannah Taylor
Originated by Capstone Global Library
Printed and bound in China by South China Printing Company Ltd

15 14 13 12 11
10 9 8 7 6 5 4 3 2 1

Library of Congress Cataloging-in-Publication Data
Thomas, Isabel, 1980-
  Painting / Isabel Thomas.—1st ed.
    p. cm.—(Start with art)
  Includes bibliographical references and index.
  ISBN 978-1-4329-5018-7 (hardcover)—ISBN 978-1-4329-5025-5 (pbk.) 1. Painting—Technique—Juvenile literature. I. Title.
  ND1146.T48 2011
  750—dc22   2010042657

Acknowledgments
We would like to thank the following for permission to reproduce photographs: Alamy Images pp. 6 (© Hemis/Chagall®/© ADAGP, Paris and DACS, London 2011), 7 (© Stock Italia), 14 (The Art Gallery Collection); © Capstone Publishers pp. 20, 21, 22, 23 – background, 23 – surface (Karon Dubke); Corbis pp. 4 (Free Agents Limited), 9, 13, 23 – Imagine (Christie's Images), 10 (The Gallery Collection), 16; Shutterstock pp. 5 (© Juriah Mosin), 8, 23 – silk (© Adam Gryko), 11 (Lauren Jade Goudie), 12 (© CYC), 23 – gallery (© Shamleen), 23 – mural (© Manuel Fernandes), 23 – palette (© Perkus), 23 – shades (© Dariusz Gudowicz); The Art Archive pp. 18 (São Paulo Art Museum Brazil/Dagli Orti), 19 (Minneapolis Institute of Fine Art/Superstock); The Bridgeman Art Library pp. 15 (Van der Heydt Museum, Wuppertal, Germany), 17 (Mellon Coll., Nat. Gallery of Art, Washington DC, USA).

Front cover photograph of Blue Fox, 1911 (oil on canvas) by Franz Marc (1880–1916) reproduced with permission of The Bridgeman Art Library (Van der Heydt Museum, Wuppertal, Germany). Back cover photograph of a girl painting reproduced with permission of Shutterstock (© Juriah Mosin). Back cover photograph of a paint palette reproduced with permission of Shutterstock (© Adam Gryko).

Every effort has been made to contact copyright holders of material reproduced in this book. Any omissions will be rectified in subsequent printings if notice is given to the publisher.

Contents

Some words are shown in bold, **like this**. You can find out what they mean by looking in the glossary.

What Is a Painting?

A painting is a picture made
with paints.

Some paintings are thousands of
years old.

A person who makes paintings is called an artist.

You can be an artist, too!

Where Can I See Paintings?

People like to look at paintings.

You can often see paintings in a museum or **gallery**.

Paintings are all around you, too.
Look for paintings outdoors.

This **mural** is painted on a building
in Italy.

What Do People Use To Make Paintings?

Artists mix paints on a **palette** to make different colors.

They dip brushes in the paint and then start painting.

People paint on paper, canvas, and other **surfaces**.

This Chinese picture is painted on **silk**.

How Do People Make Paintings?

Artists make paintings in different ways.

Most paintings have lines, shapes, and colors.

Dripping, flicking, and splattering paint makes an exciting picture.

Does this painting make you think about moving or staying still?

What Do People Paint?

Some artists paint pictures of things that they see.

They paint people, animals, places, and objects.

Some artists paint made-up
things, too.

This artist **imagined** a picture and
used painting to show us her ideas.

What Can Paintings Show?

Paintings can show us what
something looks like.

This artist copied the shapes
and colors of a real rabbit.

Paintings do not have to look real.
A fox is not really purple!

Why do you think the artist painted
this fox purple?

How Can Paintings Show Feelings?

Shapes and lines can make us feel different things.

Swirls of paint show us these stars in the night sky.

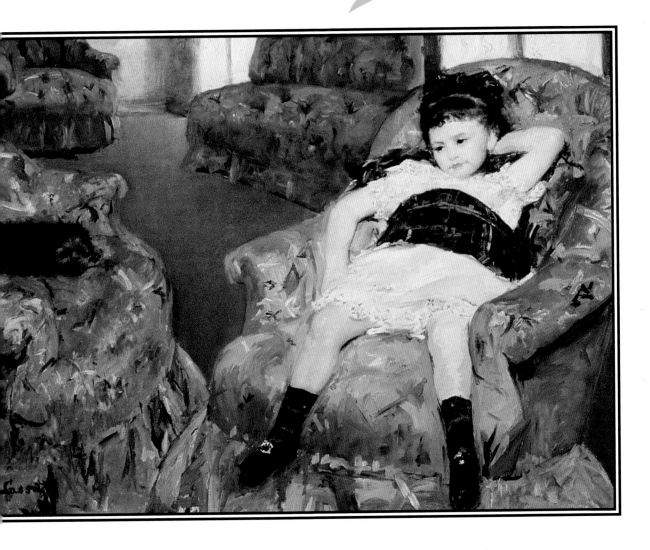

Artists use colors to show feelings, too.

Different **shades** of blue tell us this girl
is feeling sad.

What Can Paintings Tell Us?

Paintings can tell us how people lived in the past.

These little boys were painted 250 years ago. Do boys wear clothes like this today?

Paintings can tell us what life is like in other places.

This artist painted pictures of life on an island called Tahiti.

Start To Paint!

Look at the picture of the fox on page 15, and other paintings by Franz Marc.

1. Collect pictures of your favorite animal or look at real animals.

2. Plan your painting. Use a piece of chalk to draw the shapes that make up an animal.

3. Now paint your animal. You do not have to use its real colors.

4. You could choose colors that show if the animal is sad, happy, fierce, shy, or excited.

5. Decide whether to use a color for the **background**.

6. Display your picture in an animal **gallery**!

Glossary

background part of a picture that shows what is behind the thing being painted

gallery place where art is displayed for people to look at

imagine make things up in your head

mural painting on a building or wall

palette special board where an artist mixes paints

shades different kinds of one color. Light red and dark red are different shades of red.

silk fine, soft material made by silkworms

surface something that an artist paints on, such as paper, canvas, silk, or wood

Find Out More

Book

Thomas, Isabel. *Painting (Action Art).*
Chicago: Heinemann-Raintree, 2005.

Websites

See more paintings by Franz Marc on this Website:
www.ibiblio.org/wm/paint/auth/marc/

On this Website, you can try creating your own work of art in the style of
Jackson Pollock: www.jacksonpollock.org

You can explore portrait paintings on this Website:
www.museumnetworkuk.org/portraits/

Index